COZY CONVERSATIONS FOR CHRISTIAN COUPLES

NIKICHA CHARLES

© 2018 Divine Works Publishing
ALL RIGHTS RESERVED

All rights reserved. No part of this publication may be reproduced, stored in a retrieval system, or transmitted in any form or by any means, electronic, mechanical, photocopying, recording or otherwise without the prior permission of the publisher or in accordance with the provisions of the Copyright, Designs, and Patents Act 1988 or under the terms of any license permitting limited copying issued by the Copyright Licensing Agency.

The views expressed in this work are solely those of the author and do not necessarily reflect the views of the publisher, the publisher hereby disclaims any responsibility for them.

ISBN-13: 978-0-9996047-7-9 (paperback)

Published by:
Divine Works Publishing
Royal Palm Beach, Florida USA
www.divineworkspublishing.com
561-990-BOOK (2665)

DEDICATION

I want to dedicate this book to my amazing children, D'Andre, Devon, Dylan. I have no idea why God chose me to be your mom, but I promise to give you the best life ever. I want you three to know that everything I do is for you; you guys have given me so much joy and happiness. While I write you sit there with me and tell me how proud you are of me. Thank you for all my foot rubs and amazing laughs. Life would be empty without you three, who wants an empty life? I love you with all of me and I promise to keep on writing and keep being your super mommy. Life will be great for you guys because I will always give you the best of me and the best life. This one goes out to you Bubba, Papa, and Pa. I hope to make you proud and never let you down. Love you Kings!

And, to my Sweetie Sweets Semaj, who is also a part of my clan; you have been at my hip since you were born. I wasn't blessed to birth a daughter and even though I call you sister, you are like the little girl I never had. You are a joy and one of my biggest critics, I also dedicate this book to you, I've never missed any events concerning you and you have ALWAYS made me a priority in your life. Thank you for having those talks with the boys and keeping secrets from me and helping them in this phase of life. I love you Sweets. This ones also for you...

ACKNOWLEDGMENTS

Of course, this work would not have been possible without the help of a number of people. My heartfelt thanks go out…

To My Heavenly Father, who created me with a gift, who gave me an idea, who birthed purpose in me and who keeps on forgiving me no matter what I do or how many times I fall. Thank you for giving me you.

To my Pastors/Parents Dr. James and Jacqueline Wright, for being the greatest push in my life, for never leaving me out there alone, and for always believing in me. You saw something in me that I still don't see. I appreciate your desire to want more for me and your honesty has helped me conquer life with no fear. I write because you said to me "Nikicha, you are something special."

To my mentor Corinthian Pierre, you give me sound advice and your footsteps guide me without you knowing.

To My Mother Margaret Gabriel, my rock, my girl shut up, and writes, I love you and thank you for taking care of us in the hardest of times. You are the true definition of strength.

To my Editor Belinda John and Divine Works Publishing, from the moment I handed over this manuscript you have made my heart smile, thank you for believing in this book and helping me to give it life.

TABLE OF CONTENTS

CHAPTER ONE 1
Mrs. Insecure

CHAPTER TWO 11
The Aggressor

CHAPTER THREE 17
Dispelling 2 Common Myths

CHAPTER FOUR 23
The Lover

CHAPTER FIVE 27
The Choker

CHAPTER SIX 31
Mr. Can't Get it Right

CHAPTER SEVEN 35
Early Mornings/Late Nights

CHAPTER EIGHT 39
Can I Watch?

FINAL THOUGHTS 43

INTRODUCTION

Someone recently asked me what I enjoy doing, and because I am a Christian woman, I found it difficult to explain to this person what I'm *really* passionate about. It seems these days people judge you for every little thing that doesn't add up to what *they* think a "Christian" should exemplify. So, I expressed to her that I'm passionate about writing. She seemed impressed with my reply, but what I didn't say is that I am passionate about writing stories that excite people to be open in their relationships.

I'd like for my stories to become a conversation piece for couples struggling to express how they feel about their intimate moments. My stories will definitely excite you in ways you probably didn't know you could be excited. Ultimately, you'll become more comfortable with discussing sex with your partner after reading this book. These stories will in fact allow you to see how being open and talking about what you want during sex can help save a marriage.

How will your spouse really ever know what you want if you never express it to them?

This book is not limited to married couples, but singles can also use this book to help open up communication before marriage. Regardless where you may be in your relationship status it is my heart that you continue to walk according to the way God has commanded you to.

Now before we continue, understand that I was married for ten years and so I'm not only writing from a single woman's perspective, but also through the eyes of a married woman. Some may say, "well if you know so much, why then are you divorced?" Well I was open in my marriage—we both were—but other things made us grow apart. So let's get back to reading.

I've also been hesitant in writing this book, because I understand the controversy it may bring. I'm no less of a Christian than you are; I'm still saved and I love the Lord, and I like to write about things that help bring excitement to the average marriage and possibly help save a marriage or two.

Nothing in this book indicates that you should sin or step outside of your marriage. This book is designed to simply open your imagination and help you be free to express what you feel to your spouse. Sex is amazing in itself, but can become extraordinary once we aren't ashamed to share what we like and what we don't like.

Learning to be intimate in conversation first can impact your love making experience, yet many struggle with this first step. I pray that this book helps at least one couple and also helps single people to understand that it's ok to be open, to be free, and to want more than just a night of sex, but to ensue passion, intimacy, romance and to cherish every experience you have with the one you love to always make it a night to remember.

Thank you for purchasing. I hope you enjoy. Let go of what you think this book is about and come take this journey with me.

Let your imagination run wild….

CHAPTER ONE

Mrs. Insecure

They call me Stacy, I was born in a loving, secure and stable home with both parents and there wasn't much I wanted for in life. I was taught to always speak when spoken to, never lie, and to always do good to people. I graduated top of my class and married a very influential man. We had a great way of communicating and we laughed often. I felt like he was the man God designed to walk this earth with me. Although I married, I have always had this independence about myself. I never asked him for anything, which was my way of letting him see that if he ever decided to leave me that I could definitely stand on my own. He was deep into biblical studies and he was intrigued with the things of God and I absolutely loved that about him. I'm guessing you're saying to yourself, "this sounds like the perfect marriage". Well, everything was perfect-- except for the sex. It was like everytime he asked for it my body cringed, I couldn't explain it. I believed I was attracted to him and I knew I didn't want any other man, but I loathed sex with him. This became a real issue for us, because he began noticing. I remember him telling me "babe, I can feel when you tense up, what am

I doing wrong?" It reached the point where he stopped asking me for sex. I felt so bad. I loved my husband but I didn't love sex with my husband.

When I first met Stacy, I wanted her to help me understand why she wasn't comfortable with sex, so we decided to have a girls day. We talked for a while. In getting to know Stacy I began to understand where her dilemma stemmed from. You see, Stacy wasn't comfortable with the way she looked. Although Stacy was independent she was also insecure. When you are insecure it translates in the bedroom. Stacy never wanted the lights on, she never wore seductive clothing, and she never initiated anything.

If you're a Stacy, it's time to put her to death. Men don't like a woman who is insecure in the bedroom, and women don't like an insecure man either. If you don't like you, change it, but don't make him or her suffer because of what you feel.

I took stacy to a store, yes a lingerie store, all the deep ones put the book down now cause things are about to get heated... When we first got there she seemed uncomfortable, I could sense her tensing up, I laughed so hard, because I wasn't taking her in there to purchase anything "yet" but to merely help her become comfortable with sex... if Stacy wasn't comfortable with how she looked, I knew she would never be ok with sex, and so the lingerie was more to for her than for him, to help her feel more sexy so that she could get rid of the tension surrounding sex with her husband.

Ladies it is ok to be sexy, in every way. Men when you wake up next to your woman everything about her should say stay in bed baby. Sometimes it takes more than just the usual sex to keep your mate only wanting you. Sex can get boring and routined.

Do me a favor, if you're married pose this question to your spouse. "Has sex been boring?" If the answer is "yes", it's time to do something different. Ultimately you want your man or woman to leave home wishing they could stay.

Now let's get back to Stacy, while in the store I begin to show her how to open up her creativity and the different things that can be very pleasurable to her and her mate. Of course that day Stacy wouldn't purchase anything, but she was open. Still very uncomfortable with the store we decided to leave, but Stacy seemed ready to take this journey.

As the day progressed, we spoke about several things, Stacy decided this day would be the one in which she adopted a new way of thinking about sex. So I gave her some instructions for starting off the day tomorrow.

1: Tonight when you go home, greet him with a sensual kiss, not long but very seductive. What this does is stimulate his mind, it tells a man that you've been thinking about him all day. A normal kiss is expected but that slow steady kiss is a sign of intimacy.

2: Take a bath, but turn the lights off, light some candles, and turn on some music that describes how sexy you feel. Men love a woman who believes she's sexy, who appreciates how she looks no matter her size.

3: Get out the shower and get dressed in the room while he's there and don't dry off the way you normally do. Be very sexy. Now what this does is get him thinking, he will be thinking that, (one) she has had a hell of a day or (two) I wonder if she cheating on me. So to bring his mind back into the flow of the moment, remind him of something he did while you are were dating that led to sex.

4: Make sure you caress your legs slowly and seductively as you put lotion on;

Let's pause here, because I've heard women say that it takes too long at night to get in bed when all of these things have to be done. Please ladies, put some lotion on those feet and splash on something scented, please! That's sexy. Care enough about you to do those things. Trust me, you'll thank me later. As a single woman, I did that every night and when I got married it was already a habit, I couldn't go to bed without my lotion and spray and he appreciated it. He would always say, girl you smell so good, I can hardly sleep. That's what I wanted to hear, that my scents are driving you wild even as you sleep (yep... I'm naughty and he loved it).

5: Throw on something sexy; leave the granny panties in the drawer tonight, that's not required. Get in bed, lean over, and give him a kiss that only catches the bottom lip.

One may say, this is too much, well it may be for you but for Stacy it's very appropriate. She has to become aggressive in a sexy way, she has to show him now that she is comfortable with how she looks and she enjoys sex with him. Intimacy translates those things.

Intimacy is not sex, but everything that happens before sex. Intimacy should happen all day long. Trust me, if you get that right, sex after intimacy will be explosive.

So I heard from Stacy the next day, she exclaimed, "that felt great! I didn't know how he would receive me because I'd never done these things." Then she said, when I left home, he texted me and said; have a great day sexy... So I said to Stacy, let the crazy sex begin...

I explained to her that it's important to show a man that you want him. Men hate being the aggressor all the time. Sometimes it's ok, to say when you come home I want my stuff. It's ok to be saved and say some sexy things to your man. Some may even say I want your "dick" I don't say this to be vulgar, but ask your man, its sounds way sexier than saying give me this penis. (lol). I'll be saying more than that, so get ready. It's all between you and your mate, and there's nothing wrong with that. We place way more focus on minute things than we do on making sex a unique experience each time.

Moving forward, I advised stacy all day today, we are going to be texting your husband. Now this will probably turn into sexting but it will make you comfortable with talking sexy on text rather than face to face. Sexting leaves you wanting more and a little teasing can become a whole lot of fun. Stacy was nervous but I was with her the whole step of the way.

So it began;
This is the actual conversation;
Husband: have a great day sexy
Stacy: thank you handsome
Husband: wow that's a first, thank you

Stacy: did you sleep well?

Husband: not really, tossed and turn all night.

Pause, he probably was tossing because she smelled so good but couldn't react because of the way she would tense up when he wanted sex, so he was apprehensive. Let's continue.

Stacy: oh ok, what time will you be home tonight?

This is the bait question. Why? Because he is wondering, I wonder why she wants to know that, she's never asked before.

Husband: the usual time

Stacy: Ok, I'll see you then

Stacy: I love you

Husband: I love you too

Stacy: I loved your cologne this morning btw

Husband: lol, thank you

Stacy: you should wear it tonight

Husband: to bed? Why?

Stacy: it turns me on

Husband: Stacy? You were turned on?

Stacy: lol, of course, what do you think, I don't get turned on?

Husband: I don't.

Stacy: well I do, I'm turned on now

Husband: Really? That's different

Stacy: different is good,

Husband: it is

Husband: as a matter of fact, you smelled great last night, that's why I couldn't sleep.

Stacy: oh yeah, well I was thinking of you when I put it on

Husband: really, thinking what?

Pause, so I'm on her job phone while she is about to send this next text, I told Stacy, "this is where it gets hot… and he's probably gonna want you home now." Lol, here we go.

Stacy: well it actually started when I was in the shower, I was thinking how I wanted to feel you press against me, and how I wanted to smell like something you wanted to taste.

Husband: Really? Wow..

Husband: I was really holding back, I wanted you. The way you put that lotion on was so sexy.

Stacy: at that moment I was thinking about that night you asked me to _____ (fill in the blanks), and how I was afraid, but you reassured me and said we're married baby, it's ok

Husband: you remember that? That was sexy, I love that

Stacy: Yes, it was a great night,

Husband: Didn't seem great, you seemed so tense.

Stacy: I was, but all that has changed.

Husband: I like this

Stacy: me too, and you know what else I like

Husband: what?

Stacy: when you ask me if it's your stuff

Pause, now let me help you understand; there is a some language that just turns a man on and "pussy" just maybe one of those words… when being used in the bed with your husband. Even if he's a pastor, deacon, choir member, I'm sure he likes to hear his wife say some sexy things and maybe the p word will turn him on. If you don't say it, I'm sure Sally wouldn't mind. He may act like what Sally said didn't move him, but the word "pussy" used in a sexual context turns "all" men on. Try it and you'll see his face light up, just walk up to him and say "hey handsome, you want some of this good pussy?" Immediate reaction… if you know what i mean.

Let's finish this up

Husband: you said the p word. Wow, that's so sexy; I always thought you weren't attracted to me.

Stacy: naw baby, I love everything about you.

Husband: so, we can try something new tonight?

Stacy: I'm ready….

Husband: wow, I'm so hard

Stacy: where are you?

Husband: just pulled in to work

Stacy: stay in the car, let me come help you get through the day.

Huband: what? Really? Now?

Stacy: yes, I'm on the way, just sit back and allow me to taste.
Husband: OMG!!!.

At this point the text continues, but husband was just shocked that Stacy was on her way to the office.

So Stacy gets there, gets out her car, asks him to pull to a more secluded area. So he did, she tells me when she got in the car she was really excited and that everything in her wanted to just jump on him and have sex at the moment, but that's not what I instructed her to do.

You see Stacy wasn't really into the whole foreplay stuff because she wasn't comfortable with having him in her mouth. So I said to her, you're comfortable with him penetrating your vagina but he can't put his penis in your mouth? She just looked at me. I said it is your penis right? She says yes, I said would you like to always satisfy him? She said "yes", I replied "does he provide all you desire, spiritually, sexually, physically, emotionally, financially?' she says "yes", I said girl you better satisfy that man or Sally will. Oral sex with your hubby ain't gonna kill you ladies... I began to explain to her that when you act like its killing you to do it, it makes the man feel like, dang she thinks I'm dirty. It's not a chore; but all of this is a form of affection towards your mate. It's what MEN respond to.

So Stacy said they pulled around back, she leaned him back, unzipped his pants and went to work. I screamed so loud, touchdown Stacy. She said he was laying there with this look like he had never been so pleased. Men love spontaneous acts. They think it's sexy for you to go out your way to satisfy them. He told her that all he kept thinking about all day was how sexy it was for her to drive to his job to please him. It should please you to please him. It's not always about I better get mine too. **Intimacy stimulates the mind even if you aren't being touched.** See this all started from the night before; Stacy was making love to her husband without even touching him. Everything she did triggered the sexual beast in him, so much so that he woke up thinking about how sexy she was when she went to bed. Love making should be all day long, and it doesn't have to end with having sex. **When you have the ability to touch someone without**

touching them, you have mastered the art of love making.

When Stacy got home that night she said, they made love for hours, said she was so comfortable with her body and it translated through sex. She even left the lights on. Now Stacy has a spontaneous moment with her husband almost every week. She says they have become closer and can talk about anything now. Even sex...

This is the goal for all women and men, first be comfortable with how you look and that helps you become comfortable with your sexuality. You become more comfortable with being sexy for your spouse and it translates through your body language. Love everything about your spouse and understand that spontaneous acts makes sex amazing and keeps you wanting more. Become familiar with different ways of pleasing, whether it's by sexting, oral sex, intimacy, a quickie or hours of passionate love... Stacy has been having a blast and so should you.

The Cozy Conversation

- Are you Mrs. Insecure in your relationships?

- Are you comfortable with yourself? Why or why not?

- What steps can you take now to help you feel a little sexier?

- Which of the suggestions mentioned in this chapter do you think can help your relationship become a little more open concerning sexual intimacy?

CHAPTER TWO

The Aggressor

I'm the kind of person that loves to hear people discuss what they like, sexually. It doesn't turn me on or anything, it's just amazing to see how different people are. How some enjoy one thing and others find it difficult to like. So I'm sitting in the doctor's office one day and I hear this couple arguing about something that happened the night before. So I pull out a pen and paper, which I always have, and it was interesting to hear this conversation and I also wanted to research it. Now let me help you understand this, I'm not a doctor or a college grad or a therapist and I have no degrees, but I love to write and I enjoy writing about real life situations and about erotic encounters. I can't help everyone, but I've been known to help a few.

So I hear the wife say, "I'm tired of that, why can't I be the aggressor sometimes." So I'm thinking to myself, they must both be alpha, but he won't let her take control. It is my belief that all men are born alpha but I don't think every man is. God designed men to be the head of the house and to lead their homes. So that I wouldn't jump to my own conclusion, I listened a little more. She goes on and on about how she feels as if she can't show him that she also can take charge and put him to sleep. When I heard that, immediately I began to write. Honestly, how many women sometimes just want to be the one to initiate sex and get the party started? Men have to understand that in this world we have a couple of women who possess the alpha trait. What man doesn't want his woman to come home and tell him what to do (in the bed) that is.

So, being who I am, I posed this question to another woman as well as another man. I asked them both, "in a sexual setting would you be the aggressor? If so, why or why not?" This is the response I received from the woman. "I'm not sure if I am able to be the aggressor because I have only had two partners in my lifetime and I'm 35, even though I enjoy sex, I believe I'm not experienced enough to be the aggressor and I wouldn't want to embarrass myself, and I also don't want him to think in his mind while I'm trying to be the aggressor that I look like I don't know what I'm doing, but sometimes in my mind I want to be the one that makes him scream."

Yeeeeesssss, I'm all for a man saying my name, and making his eyes roll behind his head, and his toes curl. I am into that. I'm into being in control sometimes, but if not done properly you will crash and burn. Being aggressive requires a certain kind of boldness, a certain kind of sexy, you have to be willing to forget about you and focus on the person you are trying to please. Become one with the task, commit from start to finish, no quitting, no backing down, no complaint, give it your all and don't stop until he has to basically pry you off of him. I know some men who are reading this book are secretly thinking, "Yes! this is what I need." I promise if done the right way, your man/woman will be thinking about you all day.

Men, some of you also need to be aggressive, some of you are too passive. I think women expect men to automatically be alpha and always in charge, but some aren't. Some men are just as nervous about sex. Women can be so judgemental, one wrong move and the man is the worst lover ever, now let me tell you, you can destroy a man's confidence with one word. Ladies lets not do that, especially in being married, never tear him down if he can't deliver like you want. This makes communicating a valuable part of sex with your spouse.

Again I posed this question, this time to a man. His response was, aggression is my thing, I will start it up and go until my woman receives ultimate satisfaction. He explained to me that he prides himself in pleasing. He continued on in saying that's his job, to always please. So I asked "does that arouse you, to satisfy her in every way?" He replied, "man that to me is the best part of sex, to get her to the highest point of climax, to make her say 'baby please stop, I can't take it.'"Come on ladies, I know that got you thinking, what kind of man is he? Let me just say he doesn't look like how he talk. He is very quiet, doesn't boast, doesn't brag, he doesn't have much swag, but seems like he keeps her happy, whoever she might be. Being an aggressive person doesn't have a look, you can't determine from looking at a person that they are aggressive. You can't determine from a conversation that a person is aggressive. You will only know behind closed doors (any door). Let me say this, every one that talks a good talk may only be talk. Men or women, I don't have to shout how aggressive I am in bed, shouting proves nothing. The person that ultimately knows for sure is the person you are in bed with. Be aggressive, be bold, have fun.

Moving on, this same gentlemen explained to me that even though he's the aggressor in his relationship, he doesn't like for his women to just ignore his touch. I said "explain this more", he expressed to me, and made it very clear that he wasn't speaking about his wife, but he was just talking. He said that he's heard several of his friends say that their wives/spouse do not interact during sex... wait what? I'm confused, what does that mean? He continued saying his friends would often tell him in settings like a barbershop, golfing, dinner, movies, that during sex there wives were very cold, very unaffectionate, how they'd just lay there. Hold up, hold up, wait one minute, do women really do that? If that's you, please stop that today. How dare you lay in the bed with a man that takes care of you and not give him whats due to him. Yes, I said due to him. I'm not talking in a providing sense I'm saying, if a man shows you he desires you, he kisses you in all the right places, he caresses you with his kisses, gives you multiple orgasims, treats you like you're the only woman that he wants to mount, how dare you just lay there. I would say the same to a man who gets all his needs taken care of by a woman. Unfortunately, that's not common in men, but if it is ladies, do your homework, please find out why? I'm just saying; most men find that it's difficult to not have a reaction when being touched the right way. Some women can cum, and turn over, some women can't be touched after a climax other women can fake an orgasm as well, but a real man knows the difference. That's a whole other chapter. Never ever lay there as a man is sharing his love for you by catering to your body. Even Though he's the aggressor, receive him in every way, respond to his every touch, become one with his stroke, appreciate his body, and show him you want him just as much as he wants you, never be the topic of discussion unless it's him saying, guys I'm headed home...

No matter male or female, we all should possess some level of aggression. Never let your mate wonder if you desire them. They should always know... if you haven't been aggressive at all, how about you start now with just a little... and never stop pursuing your mate with passion and romance and intimacy. In all of my stories, you will always hear me say, if you don't someone else will. That's not what you want, everyone is given a set, appreciate your set. Someone is asking, what is a set? Well I'm glad you asked, again, don't judge me as you read. A set is breast and a vagina or testicles and a penis. See about your set, so no one else will have too... Unless you are already there, go ahead and be a bit more aggressive.

The Cozy Conversation

- Who is the agressor in your relationship and would changing this pattern help bring some excitment into the bedroom?

- Are you comfortable alternating aggressive roles? Why or Why Not?

- Do you think your relationship could benefit from showing a little more agression in the bedroom?

- What discussions have you and your spouse had regarding this?

CHAPTER THREE

Dispelling 2 Common Myths

We all have a common misconception that only women develop an emotional connection through sex. I hear men talk and say that they can sleep with a woman today and feel nothing tomorrow. I also hear some women say that they also can be with a guy and walk away like nothing happened.

Myth one: Women don't want sex as much as men do...Who came up with that? Not all, but some women are just as sexual as any man. Being high nature wasn't only designed to be a manly trait. Women want sex too. I know I do... but women who enjoy sex are categorized as being fast, too hot, or a whore. I'm confused because men aren't placed in these categories. I'm not saying women should sleep with multiple people, but why can't she want sex everyday just like a man? Why is it hard to accept that women have the same desires men do? Just like you discuss sex with your boys, women do the same with their girls, maybe not married women, but single women sit in settings with friends they trust and as you walk by the slap five and say "he can get it." I'm saying all this to say everyone enjoys sex, but never think men enjoy it more than women. We just are very selective "who" we allow to enter that space where we are comfortable saying; I want it, and I want it everyday. In marriage though, it's ok to get it as much as you want.

Myth Two: Sexually, men are only physically interested and they can sleep with a woman and feel nothing… Well I beg to differ, I'm not a man, but I believe a man at first can sleep with a woman and feel nothing, but if this woman gives him something he's never had, his emotions will get involved and trust he will only want this woman. Again, I will reiterate that this next step should only be made toward your spouse.

Knowing how to please a man is vital in any relationship. If a woman gives all her attention to this man all day everyday and then sees him at the end of the week, she's already tapped into his emotions. All men love attention and being catered too. They love the fact that a woman can take time out of her day to acknowledge him in any way. All of a sudden he is calling, texting, wanting to see you, even after what he taught was just sex. All men aren't just physical. That's a myth, and a man who has vowed to you in marriage will greatly appreciate any gesture of acknowledgment.

As we go on in our discussions, I will be highlighting more of these misconceptions that have been instilled in us and keep us hindered in the bedroom.

I've come to realize that many of the reasons that we don't fully experience true intimacy with our spouses is because we have been told not to do certain things in the bedroom. Let's make this clear sex is good, it can be amazing, and if done correctly it can possibly be the best experience of your life. For a healthy marriage to flourish in intimacy and sex, you will want to kick some of your reservations out the door and open yourself up to new experiences.

I want to dive into this area of conversation for a minute. One of the most important things I think should happen in any counseling as it pertains to preparing for marriage is a conversation about what a "must" in the bedroom is considered to be and what a "deal breaker can be." This conversation is important especially for those couples who are dating to marry and who have decided to abstain from sex before marriage, why? Because they've made a decision to not engage in premarital sex, but both parties should have a clear understanding of what is expected from the other party sexually.

Be willing to have a talk about it, preferably in a setting where your pastor or whoever is doing the counseling can give guidance as needed. Be open and honest about what you need to be satisfied but also be willing to submit to what your spouse wants and need as well. If early on there is not a synchronization here, it may make intimacy and connection in the marriage difficult in the long run, therefore these conversations are critical before tying the knot.

Ultimately, the goal is to communicate, execute, and live in a fulfilling marriage. This way both parties are aware of sexual wants and desires and there is never a need to wonder.

We are often so focused on the wedding day, that we forget that sex plays a big part of what we need in order to experience intimacy and to be in covenant with the one we have vowed to spend the rest of our lives with. Ultimately, the goal is to communicate, execute, and live in a fulfilling marriage. This way both parties are aware of sexual wants and desires and there is never a need to wonder.

As we grow in the marriage we've learned to keep our lines of communication open and to never be afraid to express exactly what we want and how we want it. I believe this level of openness fosters a deep initmacy and can be one of the best parts about a relationship. It is in this cozy communication where the art of love can flourish in full effect.

The Cozy Conversation

- *Prior to reading this chapter, did you believe these myths to be true?*

- *If so, how has reading this information changed your thinking?*

- *Do you think that you can help foster a deeper emotional connection with a man by pleasing him sexually?*

- *What are your sexual likes and dislikes? Are you ready to discuss them?*

CHAPTER FOUR

The Lover

Love is a beautiful thing, however I recently heard someone say that they have never been in love. I always wondered why that is, how is it possible to go through life without ever falling for someone. What is life without love? A romantic love that is. I had to really figure that thing out because someone had to come along and make you feel beautiful, or make you feel like the queen of his life, but the real question is why can't anyone get past your wall? What happened that keeps your emotions all boxed in? What happened to make you forget what love is supposed to feel like? In the art of love, none of this is possible--love, happiness, sex, intimacy, passion, or communication-- if we don't first love ourselves. True love is something you'll never be able to run from, it pulls on you, it's something you have no control of, love grips on all the emotions you have and makes you feel like nothing can change the moment that you are in. Love is powerful, but if it is never received then it can never be returned.

A woman once said to me, Ms. Charles life owes me nothing, I'm comfortable living without love, I find peace in coming home alone. My response was then my love I'm sorry, because you have missed out on one amazing part of life, love and being in love with that one person that you can call your lover. Seems she could've been offended because in her mind she believed that sex without love was great, but if that is the case then try sex within the confines of marriage with a man that makes you forget about the horrible day you had. Try experiencing love with that one woman who knows exactly which area to kiss that takes you to a place of ecstasy, try feeling a rush, a burst of sensations when the one you love, your lover, the one who knows all of you, but accepts every inch of you, this love is not something you experience through conversation, through a one night stand, this love is formed in two people who have first learned how to be ok with who they are individually and have found everything about the one they love to be amazingly attractive.

The lover is the most amazing person to fall for because once you experience love with them, intimacy will never again be the same. It's as if that person knows everything you desire to feel without you having to ask. They know how to touch you and every touch is exoctic, erotic, sexy, and romantic. This kind of passion is beautiful. When picking a lifetime partner, get you a lover, but first you must learn to love yourself. The lover is the person who can love out of you everything you thought was wrong. The lover makes you crave intimacy, and makes you think about them most of the day. The lover makes you smile when sex is over and your mind goes back to specifics, what he did, how he did it, and how he knew to kiss you there. If you're a male you begin to think about how she positioned her body the right way, at the perfect time, to give you the right access and all of a sudden the lover leaves you wanting more.

For me, I can not go through life without feeling this kind of love and attraction. I am such a poetic person and every moment in my life I want to be like a movie, I want life, love, sex, intimacy, talking and breathing his/her air to always be beautiful. What exactly is life without love? No one should ever live this life with out love. The key is to first become the lover you desire, live as the lover, and then you can fully accept the lover...

The Cozy Conversation

- Do you have what it takes to become the lover?

- Have you ever experienced this kind of romance?

- The key to being The Lover, is knowing exactly what your partner responds to and doing those things passionately. How can you improve in this area?

- What discussions have you and your spouse had regarding this?

CHAPTER FIVE

The Choker

You'll be amazed at the things I hear while working at a hair salon. This happened a while back when I was just about to graduate from school. These ladies were talking about how they enjoyed being choked during sex. No joke... Now at my age I'm thinking why anyone would want to be choked, like that's dangerous.

So I thought! I finally found the courage to ask a woman about this and what she said made me re-think some things-- it seems she enjoyed being choked by her husband and it turned her on. Wait, so you're telling me that being choked turns you on? This is where the conversation got interesting. Apparently it's not a choke with the intent to hurt, it's sensual and sexy and seductive with just the right amount of pressure. Supposedly at the peak of climax it adds to the experience and makes the climax more memorable. I'm not sure what tickles your fancy, but I wouldn't mind being choked by my husband to experience another level of climax. Some say that this kind of climax is one you will think about all day, visualizing your partners hand around your neck as he looks deep into your eyes and says call me daddy. Wow, what an experience! Are we afraid of these experiences? Are we comfortable with the same things? Is life just supposed to be normal in the confines of a bedroom? Why is the choker frowned upon? I asked these questions to women in different setting, church, gym, work and it seems that women feel that the idea of being choked is degrading. One said so in order to feel a different kind of climax, a more erotic climax, I have to let my husband abuse me?? In my mind, I thought SEE... this is why men aren't comfortable expressing what they really want. So a husband can't say, baby when you orgasm can I choke you because it turns me on? Remember, I said sensually... Is that degrading? Really! Like, let this man choke you, let him freely express himself to you with the desire of ultimately pleasing you. I mean who wouldn't want ultimate satisfaction with their mate.

Now ladies, don't you choke, that doesn't seem to work both ways. While having this conversation, one lady screams "whatever he wants to do to me, I better be able to do to him." I'm not sure if a man would allow you to choke him, seems a bit unorthodox. I mean, me personally, I can't see myself choking my husband, seems to take the man out of the man. Some things your husband does to you, you will never be able to do to him. Relax ma, take a deep breath, and let him gently put his hands around your neck, curve your back and enjoy the ride. I promise you'll enjoy that moment of pure ecstasy. Thank me later. I want the doubting, stuck in between yes or no woman to understand that a man that loves you will never want to hurt you in bed, but he finds pleasure in pleasing you, and for that we should be willing to return the favor. I'm not suggesting that every man wants to participate in this kind of intimacy, but if he did, would he ever be able to share that with you or would he think that you would find him to be a man that wants to degrade his women and therefore keep silent and keep his desires unmet? This type of communication is critical for the growth of your relationship.

I'll tell you what, I'm the kind that would insist that my husband enjoy all of me, I'll be the one to say "choke me daddy, make me think about you all day, make me want more. I want to explore everything beautiful with my king." I want to never leave him thinking "what if". What if, will only be in his mind if he's preparing to ask "hey bae what if we tried this". Life is about making love beautiful and falling daily and becoming your spouse's best partner in life. Make every encounter count. Make love a movie, every time.

The Cozy Conversation

- *Have you ever experienced this before?*

- *Would you like to and why?*

- *What other creative things would you like to experiment in the bedroomwith?*

CHAPTER SIX

Mr. Can't Get it Right

I know it seems like I've been going in on the ladies, I know, I know, it's just that most women have so many stipulations when it comes to sex. They either require so much or won't allow enough. I just want women to be a bit more open minded. This section though, has to do with the men who can't get it right. Like at what point do you listen to your women say "no baby, not like that."

You all should know by now that I love to tell a story. So, here it is, I am simply having girl talk with a coworker, "people like to talk to me" and she begins to express her frustration because her husband can't seem to hit it right, I'm like so tell him. After I said that, this conversation lasted hours. She begin to express how for many years she said to him that what he was doing wasn't satisfying her and she said she was willing to teach him. I was like "ohhh no my love, never tell a man, that you can teach him how to please you, simply do it." There is always a way to get a man to do exactly what you want without making him feel like he has no idea of what you need. She goes on to say, he is the kind of man who is stubborn and won't accept direction. So I offered, "let's try to help him." I asked in the heat of the moment, when he does do something right, do you respond? She replies "no, I just lay there". Big mistake, how will he ever know what you like if you don't respond? Say something! Make some noise, moan, and move around. The more you do that the more he'll pay attention to your body language. Then pleasing you or knowing what you like helps him do what you want without you ever saying one word. Mr. Can't Get it Right will get it right if you moan right. It has to get to a point where you say what you need without making him feel less than.

So in the event that Mr. Can't Get it Right has no clue how to get it right, and what is mentioned above hasn't been helping, what then do we do? Well I'm still working on that. You see men are easily torn down and any little thing said to them can break who they are and then all of a sudden a simple talk about what you feel can make him insecure and having an erection becomes a whole other issue. We don't want that, we never want to tear our Mr. down. My struggle here is if you don't find a way to communicate this, then you risk exploring opportunities of really feeling that explosive kind of love. So my suggestion is this, simply try the first option and if that doesn't work and you think your mate can handle a conversation, them have it but be prepared for whatever comes along with that. If that doesn't seem like the best option for you, then involve a third party. Someone who can help resolve this for you without it causing an issue in your home. The reason to try is because if you're not satisfied then sex will become a chore and not something you enjoy. And you should always enjoy sex all the time, everytime you have it. Mr. Can't get it right, has to get it right.

It's a must... please get it right so we can sleep good at night.

The Cozy Conversation

- Are you able to tell your partner if they haven't quite got it right?

- How can you assist them in getting in right?

- Are you able to accept when they say you haven't gotten it right?

- Are you willing to open up and communicate about what these things might be?

CHAPTER SEVEN

Early Mornings/Late Nights

What is this argument that couples have about what time is the best time to have relations? Are we really discussing this? Is there really a such thing? Well of course there is. The craziest thing is to find yourself arguing about "when" to have sex. Me personally, I have no preference sex is sex no matter the time of day. I have a friend guy though, that will not under any circumstances have sex if the sun is up. He says and I quote "something in me just doesn't want it." In my mind I'm like wow, I wonder if there are couples who have these issues. Like what if the husband wants it only at night and the wife wants it only in the morning, then what is the compromise? What do we do? Is a person only turned on at the moment they want it? How does one deal with this? See why these cozy conversations are so imperative to have early on?

Well, I found a couple that mastered this situation. The wife said she didn't like when the husband woke her up in the morning because she worked so late at night, but she felt it was wrong to tell him no. She said for a while she would turn over and say "bae please,

I'm tired, or you know I work hard." So she decided she would talk to him and ask him why he only wanted to have sex in the morning, like why he wouldn't try when she got home and before she fell into a deep sleep. He replied that morning sex has always been his thing and that he is turned on by how she sleeps. He would watch her while she slept and it made him want her so much. He knew she was tired so he would let her sleep first and when he was at his horniest he would wake her and on top of that he really preferred morning sex.

So this is what they did, they had this conversation first, communicated the pros and cons, and came to an agreement. He would be able to get what he wanted and so would she. Sex was a must between the hours of 12a -3a late night, early morning. He wins and so does she. Now she told me that this made sex so much better because her mind was set to know that at any time between the hours of 12-3 she knew sex was happening, and that was exciting to her. She said they've been married for 33 years and they have lots of sex because they came to a compromise. So, no matter what your preferred time is, make it work with your spouse. Me, personally, I love sex any time of day. I'd make myself available whenever he was and I'm sure he would appreciate that. We shouldn't argue about timing. Sex again, is not a chore. Don't pencil me in (well if you're using the right pencil I don't mind... wink...). Hopefully it's not a pencil though... ok, back to what I was saying, find the time that works for you and your spouse and be willing to compromise. You should never tell your mate no, for no reason at all. Early morning or a late night, doesn't matter, just work it out...

The Cozy Conversation

- Do you or your partner have a prefered time for sexual intimacy?

- Do you presently have a conflict regarding timing?

- Are you able to come to a creative compromise where both parties are satisfied if a time conflict exists?

- If you do have a conflict, what are some options you can try, list at least 3.

CHAPTER EIGHT

Can I Watch?

Ok, see maybe you, yes you, should stop reading here, lol. Possibly too late, but it gets a little more controversial at this point. Can I watch? Simply means exactly what you think. Here we talk about is it ok to watch your spouse masturbate while in the room with you? I have not found any scriptural reference that prohibits a married couple from putting on a show for their spouse. The bible does mention in Hebrews 13:4 that marriage is honorable and the bed is undefiled. So, what I do with my husband in my bedroom isn't wrong. If it is, I really don't mind being corrected, but I think that if my husband asked me to touch myself while he watched I would not decline. I think that to a man that can be a very sexy and exciting time. Just for him to sit and watch and then at the right moment take over and finish what he asked me to start. Man that's sexy. For him to say "baby, get her ready for me." Oh yeah, that's sexy. Is there really something wrong with a woman saying, "I'm on my way home daddy, pull it out and wake big daddy up for me." That'll mess his mind up. What exactly is wrong with that? I'm not thinking about anyone else but my husband and I know he'll be thinking about me. I've heard women say that they won't ever do that, and I'm like "oh ok, but I will." And I know he'll love it. No one said to finish, but let him see that once and he'll never be able to get that picture out his mind. He comes home walks into the room and there you are middle of the bed, legs open, saying teasing him, touching her and saying, I've been waiting on you to finish this for me. If that ain't sexy then I don't know what is. Trust me, I put the s in sexy. Everyone won't agree, but talk about it, ask him/her can you watch. I guarantee some will be like "oh wow, I thought you were too saved to do that, or I thought you would get upset if I asked." To be sexy for your spouse in your room in your bed can't possibly be a sin. Men live and say "bae open those legs and get to work so daddy can slide in smooth." Let my hubby tell me that, I may slip and fall from trying to get to my bed so fast. I'm joking around, but this is a big topic in some Christian's homes, my suggestion is to get your own revelation and talk about it, and see if this is too far for you.

    I spoke to one gentleman about this and he said one of the biggest arguments he's had in his bedroom is asking for his wife to be sexier and she always replies " I ain't going to hell for you." He said Ms. Charles I didn't ask her to sing, I asked for lingerie, no panties, legs open and hands on the clit and she cried saying I was trying to turn her into a whore. My reply, what was so wrong with being a whore for you? Now they were already divorced so this is why I replied the way that I did. One thing I'll never do is discuss a spouse with another spouse, especially let a man talk to me about his wife. He can talk to his home boy or pastor. But, aren't we supposed to be the ones they lust after? The one their body craves and vice versa? I will be his whore any day of the week. I'll dress up, role play, and touch it if he likes me to. Again, It's my own belief that God wants me to satisfy my husband. If I don't... Sally will. And I promise you Sally will never do it better than me, I won't give her opportunity to. I will master making him happy and every time he touches me I'll be doing something to mess his mind up. Don't get bored in the bedroom. Don't let people tell you what you should and shouldn't do in your room, the place where covenant takes place. Touch it, lick it, rub it, stick it, do all you want to it, as long as it doesn't violate the word of God and each other, and it won't bring pain... So, can I watch? Yes, you can...

The Cozy Conversation

- *How do you feel about this topic of watching?*

- *Do you know how your partner feels about watching or being watched? Have you had the conversation?*

- *What can you do to implement or enhance your sex life by incorporating some of these suggestions?*

- *What, if anything, is stopping you?*

FINAL THOUGHTS

Although, a lot of what I said was shared in a humorous tone, realistically life can be amazing, love can be beautiful, and enjoying your spouse can be something fulfilling. We should never be so stuck in our ways that we don't even listen to the person laying next to us. I'm aware that some may not agree with some of the things I said in this book, and that's fine. I don't expect everyone to relate with all of the stories or chapters written in this book. I used some extremes to help encourage the dialogue and begin the conversations that so many struggle with silently. My desire was to show that love making doesn't have to be the same experience each time and that it's ok to say and do certain things, out of the usual, in the bedroom with your spouse. I also do understand that some will take this book and apply it and have very amazing experiences with their spouse.

I never once suggested or encouraged in this book that anyone sin or go against what God's word deems right. I also stated that everything mentioned in this book should be done or applied between married couples because I do understand the importance of marriage and believe in its sanctity.

You may not believe it after reading this book, but I am an ordained pastor and have been for years, but I had also been the other woman to a married man; something I'm not proud of at all. However, through that experience, I learned the value of cherishing and nurturing your marriage and your intimacy. Understand that sex is about more than just a moment to release; it's about passion, commitment, communication, mind stimulation, and making a person desire you every single day. I have seen marriages fall apart because of lack of communication and fear of not being able to express what they want and how they want it.

A couple should be able to speak about everything. Nothing should be off limits, you should never be afraid to talk to the one who lies in the bed with you about anything. If you won't listen, someone else will. Your mate should be your best friend. The one you discuss everything with, even if it's sex.

I am a firm believer of having strong communication, being able to fully be you around your spouse is very important. You shouldn't have to change who you are, to be with the one you love. Adjusting may have to take place in certain areas, but that is only discovered when we are able to talk and express then we can grow together. All I'm saying is a saved Christian couple shouldn't be afraid of being open. Have a good ole' freaky time with your spouse. Enjoy each other, talk nasty, grab each other, love every inch of the one God gave you and keep your bedroom to you and your spouse. Some people will put you in hell for giving the best you have to your man/woman. Will God judge me for loving every inch of my husband?

I really hope this book helped some, I know some maybe upset, I know I'm probably being judged and that's ok. I'm not sure what will be the backlash of this book, all I know is I enjoy writing about real things that will help people who are afraid to ask questions, people who are afraid of being judged or frowned upon for wanting a better sex life in a Christian marriage. Some may say "oh pray about it, you can, but you can also just say, hey hunny, I like it better when you do it this way." For a man he can say, "not too hard or open your mouth a little." What's so wrong with that? No one is breaking any rules or going against anything in the bible. Love should be fun, sex should be great, and life should be amazing with the one you love. If this isn't something you desire, but you have read this book all the way through, then realistically this is something you do want.

I am Nikicha Charles and this is the Art of Love...

ABOUT THE AUTHOR

Nikicha Charles was born November 2, 1982 to Ms. Margaret Gabriel and Alphonse Victor and is the second oldest of 6 Children. Currently a single mother of 3, who was adopted into the Christian home of Bihsop James and Jaqueline Wright at the age of 17, Nikicha began writing poetry in high school and through the encouragement of her ex-husband (Leroy) she continued to write about all things that mattered to her. She is now purposefully pursuing her passion to help couples with intimacy and is thankful to God for every trail she treaded, every area that she failed, and for every mistake, every betrayal and every low place. "For every time I heard the words YOU CAN'T. I am proud to say I DID. I AM A PASTOR, A MOTHER, A FRIEND, and A WRITER…"

You never really know what life has in store for you until after you start living it!

www.ingramcontent.com/pod-product-compliance
Lightning Source LLC
Chambersburg PA
CBHW020431010526
44118CB00010B/527